JUST THE TIPS

MATT FRACTION
CHIP ZDARSKY

EDITOR: THOMAS K

IMAGE COMICS

JUST THE TIPS. First printing. November 2014. Copyright © 2014 Milkfed Criminal Masterminds, Inc. & Zdarsco, Inc. All rights reserved. Published by Image Comics, Inc. Office of publication: 2001 Center Street, Sixth Floor, Berkeley, CA 94704. "Just The Tips," the Just The Tips logo, and the likenesses of all characters herein are trademarks of Milkfed Criminal Masterminds, Inc. & Zdarsco, Inc., unless otherwise noted. "Image" and the Image Comics logos are registered trademarks of Image Comics, Inc. No part of this publication may be reproduced or transmitted, in any form or by any means (except for short excerpts for journalistic or review purposes), without the express written permission of Milkfed Criminal Masterminds, Inc., Zdarsco, Inc., or Image Comics, Inc. All names, characters, events, and locales in this publication are entirely fictional. Any resemblance to actual persons (living or dead), events, or places, without satiric intent, is coincidental. Printed in the USA. For information regarding the CPSIA on this printed material call: 203-595-3636 and provide reference #RICH–594047. For international rights, contact: foreignlicensing@imagecomics.com. ISBN: 978-1-63215-178-0

This book is dedicated to Chip Zdarsky, who taught me everything I know about sex — and love. And who I know would never, ever, dedicate a book to anyone or anything else but me, because we are in love, and we are partners together, forever, in all things. I love you, chum.

-Matt

This book is dedicated to Sex, the ancient god of wheat, who—wait, is that right?

-Chip

Foreword by President Barack Hussein Obama

People of America and people of soon-to-be-America, prepare to fuck ... well.

In this collection of sexual tips lies everything you'll need to know in order to suck, fuck and lick your partner high above where the eagles soar. Now, literally everyone I know warned me to not attach my name to this book, but if there's one thing I've learned from being president over the last eleven years, it's that you gotta be you. And President Obama hungers for sexual knowledge.

What these gentlemen have done is nothing short of miraculous. For dozens of years people have been having sex poorly, and with this book Matt and Chip have burst into all of our bedrooms with their greasy, tender hands, and guided our average bodies to a bunch of orgasms.

If you take offence to what they've done here, well, I immediately pardon that offence, as is my power. So you may as well just enjoy what you're about to read.

Obama

President Obama

SEX TIPS for you and yours

Let your man know you're thinking about him all day long by using digital technology to constantly maintain surveillance of his erection.

Try sex toys to add a little variety in the bedroom. Maybe a slutty Optimus Prime?

When making love, whisper in her ear, "god is dead," to let her know that it's OK to get real freaky.

Don't forget to thank your sexual partner with a "Thanks for the fuck" greeting card or a replenishing fruit basket.

EROTICA to read to your illiterate lover

Janice wanted to fuck the vampire. More than any werewolf or ghost. The thought consumed her. She unzipped Gary's dirty jeans to unleash his undead, alabaster peener and was stunned at what she saw.

"It ... it's so small and soft," she blurted gently, her super-moist mouth suddenly drying up as if a dicksponge was recently in it. Gary explained.

"It has been too long since I've fed, and so my body cannot spare the extra blood required for an erection. Perhaps if I feasted on you for a bit...?"

Janice nodded, willing to sacrifice anything for a crazy dicking, and Gary plunged his teeth-boners into her thick neck, taking a good gallon of the yummy blood. Janice was pretty weak, but she still went straight for his flesh stake, which was now hard as a rock.

"Oh. It's ... still so small."

"Yes. Sorry."

PICK-UP LINES to pick up while in lines

Ooh, boy, are you Todd McFarlane? Because I want to see your balls.

Ooh, boy, are you Reynaud's Syndrome? Because my nipples are hard.

Ooh, boy, are you Bruce Willis and Demi Moore? Because I wish you worked out.

Ooh, boy, do you like Isaac Hayes? Because I'm talkin' about shaft.

Ooh boy are you Joe Montana? Because I am wide open.

Ooh, boy, are you AP English 5? Because I thought you were supposed to be hard.

Ooh, boy, are you San Juan Capistrano? Because... swallows?

Ooh, boy, are you Dave Matthews? Because I am a huge fan.

Ooh, boy, are you my cat? Because I want you always in my bed, making a lot of goddamn noise.

EROTICA to get your labia crazy hard

Ellen had never known the touch of a woman before and was awfully nervous. But Kasha knew this, and tried to make it easier for her. She slowly slid her hand down Ellen's nice pantsuit and began a light fingering. Ellen moaned reservedly.

"It's OK, Ellen," purred Kasha. "Just think of my fingers as little dicks." This reassured Ellen, who had a long history of loving dicks. Kasha moved south, slipping that pantsuit right off and folding it nicely before tearing Ellen's underwear to shreds, revealing her before-this-moment-heteropussy.

"Don't worry, Ellen. I'm just using my tonguedick on you." Kasha began teasing her ladybits with that tonguedick, and it didn't take long for Ellen to orgasm like a seal flopping around on a hot rock.

Kasha moved back up and kissed Ellen on the mouth. Ellen pulled back, with a quizzical look.

"Why does your breath taste like cum?"

"Oh shit. I tonguecame in your muff. Are you on the pill?"

HOT POSITIONS

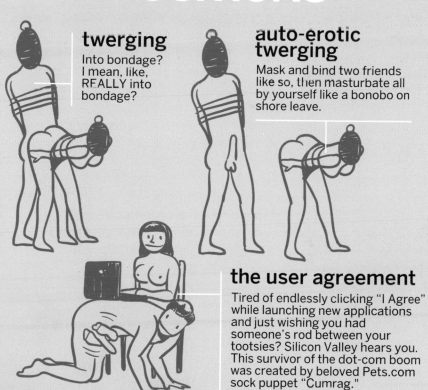

twerging

Into bondage? I mean, like, REALLY into bondage?

auto-erotic twerging

Mask and bind two friends like so, then masturbate all by yourself like a bonobo on shore leave.

the user agreement

Tired of endlessly clicking "I Agree" while launching new applications and just wishing you had someone's rod between your tootsies? Silicon Valley hears you. This survivor of the dot-com boom was created by beloved Pets.com sock puppet "Cumrag."

TRUE TALES OF FINDING PORN **from our erotic readers**

"We found the literature open on a pile of limestone. Swank magazine. Centerfold. Penetration. Just feet away, another lay open face down. Not far from that magazine lay another and another. Like a trail of bread cums, they led to a boxcar sitting amongst the rubble. The door to said boxcar, invitingly ajar with books bursting from the entrance.

"Blinded by curiosity we entered the boxcar to find a mountain of porn. We stepped onto the magazines which sounded like a pile of autumn leaves. After the astonishment of our discovery wore off, our eyes adjusted to the sunlight entering the boxcar. All four of us looked up together to see eight homeless men sitting on couches at the other end." **-Burns**

"I found my unprecedented THIRD phone abandoned this year. I opened it up and found a folder named "boobs"— which was empty—and a single penis." **-Nick**

HOT POSITIONS

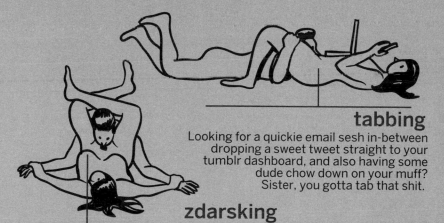

tabbing

Looking for a quickie email sesh in-between dropping a sweet tweet straight to your tumblr dashboard, and also having some dude chow down on your muff? Sister, you gotta tab that shit.

zdarsking

you're USELESS chip just fucking USELESS this is what USELESS FUCKS fucking GET chip this is what you GET

the li'l hitler

Smother them against your landing strip—the thrashing and struggling, along with the little bit of pube right under their nose, makes whoever's dining out at YOUR V look an awful lot like a Li'l Hitler. Hey do you think that's where they got the name from?

HOT POSITIONS

bunting

Tap his balls lightly just before the moment of orgasm and watch as pleasure and pain combine to create a confused ejaculation that dribbles away from home rather than flying for the outfield fences.

scooting

Created for the XXX Games by the sexual sportsmen at ESPN (Extra Sexy Positions Niiiiiice), scooting combines the adrenalized excitement of motocross with the erotic magnetism of that old Inchworm thing you used for tooling around your driveway when you were like four.

ball boobing

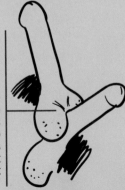

Four balls, two sacks, one shaft, let's party! Using the natural décolletage of a gentleman's dongboobs, slide up and down a penis until you either get super into it or start laughing too much.

PICK-UP LINES to get you some sex before we make you best at sex

Girl, are you Mark Ruffalo? Because I think you're widely underappreciated.

Girl, they call me Jude Law, because I am in everything.

Girl, are you Mark Harmon? Because even my mom wants to sleep with you.

Girl, are you a stripper? Because I would pay you money to take off your clothes and pretend to like me.

Girl, are you the filmography of Rainer Werner Fassbinder? Because I find you challenging but worth it.

Girl, are you the Susan G. Komen Foundation? Because everywhere I go you got me thinking about boobs.

Girl, do cheesy lines work on you? Because there's a new Nicholas Sparks movie opening.

Girl, are you Italian? Because I want-a to-a touch-a your boobs-a.

DIRTY TALK

for when you're in the throes of passion or pre-thro

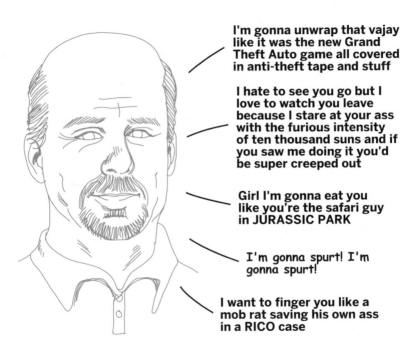

I'm gonna unwrap that vajay like it was the new Grand Theft Auto game all covered in anti-theft tape and stuff

I hate to see you go but I love to watch you leave because I stare at your ass with the furious intensity of ten thousand suns and if you saw me doing it you'd be super creeped out

Girl I'm gonna eat you like you're the safari guy in JURASSIC PARK

I'm gonna spurt! I'm gonna spurt!

I want to finger you like a mob rat saving his own ass in a RICO case

SEX TIPS
for reading around the campfire

Sending your partners sexy photos will get their engines all revved up. If you're shy, alternate with pics of celebrities looking UNsexy to make you seem even sexier by comparison.

Rub beloved film star and rapper Ice Cube all over your partner's body.

Read her 50 Shades of Grey in bed because women find a sense of humor very sexy.

Ladies! Entice your man by shaving off all your pubic hairs and sprinkling them on the bed like rose petals.

SEX TIPS

you won't find in a textbook unless this becomes a textbook I guess

Fellas! Looking for the one sex move guaranteed to drive her wild? So are we! Write to JUST THE TIPS, care of Image Comics, 2001 Center Street, Sixth Floor, Berkeley, CA 94704.

Carnal inspiration can come from anywhere. Try going to the zoo and imagine what animals look the hottest when they fuck. Did you guess 'giraffes'? You're right!

Surprise him with this spicy little maneuver: stick a pinky in his butthole. Not your pinky. Like—someone else's. You can get one off the internet or something I bet.

SEX TIPS

to win gold at the sexlympics

There're over 50 collections of Garfield strips and not a single one is about fucking so maybe put them away Chip.

Use all senses when making love: sight, smell, hearing, touch, taste and the all-important ESP to figure out if this guy is going to make you cum or not.

If you're busy, make sure to schedule sex. Especially to coincide with the alignment of Mars and Jupiter during the secret 13th month of Judastober, bringing about the End Times and freeing up tons of time for doing it.

Fishing can be really erotic, I guess. I mean, there's a pole, and rubber boots. So, uh, yeah, go for a fish 'n' fuck.

SEX TIPS for the modern sexer

Before making "love," prepare a hot bath together. Stock your bathroom with fluffy towels, fragrant soaps, tasteful candles, high thread-count washcloths, elegant faucet fixtures, classy potpourri, and more, all available online now at bedbathbeyond.com. Bed Bath and Beyond: Helping You Fuck In Your Bathroom Better.™

Get back in touch with your inner horny teenager. Take her to a steamy rated-R movie, sit in the back row together, then try fingerblasting her through her pants pocket.

Don't "have" sex, "give" sex.

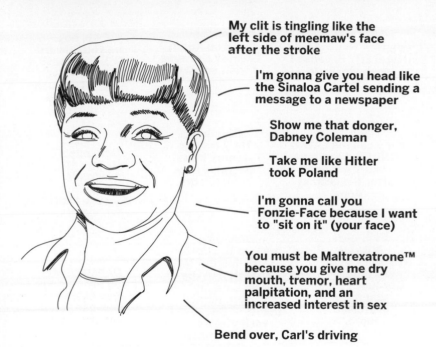

PICK-UP LINES because put-down lines won't get you laid

Ooh, boy, are you that Neutral Milk Hotel EP? Because I wish you were longer.

Ooh, boy, are you Adam Levine? Because I wish you were dead.

Ooh, boy, are you Edward Scissorhands? Because I've never seen such a manicured bush.

Ooh, boy, they call me LAW & ORDER, because I always get good after the second dong.

Ooh, boy, they call me Jeremy Irons, because I am cold and dry.

Ooh, boy, are you an academic paper? Because I am cold and dry.

Ooh, boy, are you restraint of pen and tongue? Because I wish you were exercised more.

Ooh, boy, are you the United States-led military coalition in the Middle East and/or the Syrian battle theater? Because I wish you were better defined and shorter.

Ooh, boy, are you my student loan overage? Because you'll get spent way too quickly.

MOVIE REVIEWS
pause isn't the only button getting a workout tonight

HARD-ON FINK

Directed by Joel and Ethan Boen
Starring Johnny Spurturro, Jazmine St. Cocaine, Steve Buscemi

When up-and-"cumming" pornograph writer Hard-on Fink "cums" to Hollywood to write for motion pictures, he "cums" to realize there's a lot more to the life of the mind than just cumming all over everything all the time. Like racism. And the Second World War.

8 boners out of 10

PRON: LEG-ASSY

Directed by Orson Belles
Starring Sluice Cox-Lightener, Jeff Ridges

Two video game nerds fuck a Galaga or something, then run around in weird neon body condoms, throwing Frisbees at one another's dicks for like forty-five minutes. Kind of gay? Hard to tell.

4 boners out of 10

ASK THE SEXPERTS

"The penis. How do we make it fun for all?" -Manuel

Little hats. -**Matt**

Cool sunglasses tattoo. -**Chip**

"How do you know if a girl's actually interested in you, or is just trying to be nice and is pitying you?" -Arsh

Take it from me, the guy that just had his nipple pierced on stage at a Toronto sex club—just get it over with. Ask her out, casually. And then you'll know. -**Matt**

Marry someone else and raise a family with them. If this person's interested in you, they'll let you know once they see what an amazing family you've created. -**Chip**

ASK THE SEXPERTS

I have begun dating a real sweet vegan gal. I'm trying to respect her needs, but it can be exhausting. The problem is that so many animal products are in condoms and they're tested on animals! I'm looking for options and products that you can recommend that wont make me look like a careless boyfriend when I pull them out in the bedroom. -Paul

Have a vasectomy. If you really care about this girl it's the only way. Or you could google "Vegan condoms" and choose from any of the number of certified animal-and cruelty-free condoms and lubes produced today. **-Matt**

I am unable to help here as I do not believe in cruelty-free sex. Sorry. **-Chip**

TRUE TALES OF DIDDLING YOUR STUFF from our erotic readers

"I recently spent time in Israel on a fairly large group trip, and one of our activities was spending a night in the desert. My friends and I were struck by the beauty. Its cresting dunes and vibrant sunset filled us with pure awe. Needless to say, we had to cum in it. We had to plant our seed in Israel, so that no matter where we were, we would always be connected to the Holy Land. So, after everyone else had gone to sleep, we snuck off into the night, so that we could make our small cum oasis in peace. We lay in a circle, and one by one left our mark. We didn't even require pornography, for the sheer beauty of the land around us was enough." **-Max**

"With me (and many others) masturbation started in the bath, so naturally when I got a waterproof vibrator I thought I'd get back to my roots and give my bed springs a rest. Little did I know that I didn't have the battery end screwed all the way on, so once I got pretty heated and turned on said phallic mechanism I got shocked. Yeah. I was frightened for the few seconds of realization, then shortly after laughed hysterically. I now love electricity, go figure." **-Amanda**

TRUE TALES OF FIRST TIMES from our erotic readers

"So me and the first girl I ever kissed have decided, rather suddenly, that we should have sex, like, RIGHT NOW. But, because neither of us had ever had sex before, neither of us had condoms.

A solution presents itself to us: in her house, where we were, was a bag of party balloons. And we're like, "a condom's basically just a balloon that goes on a dick, right?" Right? Right. So kneeling over her while we're both completely naked, I rip open the bag with shaking hands and they go flying everywhere, including onto her breasts. Very "American Beauty." I pick a purple- black one up, and, through a combination of her saliva and my own grim determination, we manage to get the damn thing onto my cock.

However, due to physics, biology, poor planning, the balloon would not come off over the head of my penis without causing severe pain. Finally, the girl to whom I'd lost my virginity, and whose virginity I'd just taken, agreed to just rip the thing off as fast as possible.

I had a bruise for a week, and the head of my cock was stained purple(r) for almost as long." **-Alan**

GENITALS OF THE FUTURE
PROBABLY

if you're having sex troubles. maybe wait a few years for these advances in sexology

Vaginas are fantastic, but I have some suggestions. First, clitorises should glow. It would have saved me a lot of trouble from ages 17-20. Next, and this goes for guys too, pubic hair should be softer and maybe fluffy like a pillow. And instead of just your li'l pee hole, ladies should get to have a tiny penis. Not too much that it gets in the way, but just enough that you can grab it and pee standing up with ease. Also, maybe I can suck it a bit?

balls

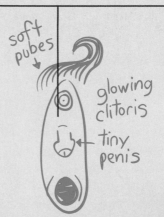

soft pubes

glowing clitoris

tiny penis

Balls. WHY ARE THEY ON THE OUTSIDE OF THE BODY? It's crazy! They're very important and easily hurt! Sure, it's nice when someone licks 'em or electrocutes them a bit but that's not worth the constant worry about slamming them in your desk drawer. So, I think they should be relocated to just under the heart, because they are just that valuable.

Penises are cool and all, but maybe instead of going soft, they can just be collapsible. That way, if a guy is losing his erection, instead of gettin' squishy, it can get a little bit shorter, but compensate with the ridges created from the collapsing! Also, maybe a tiny vagina just above the penis, for deep throatin' champs who want to give a little nose lovin'. Also, it bleeds once a month so guys can deal with that shit too.

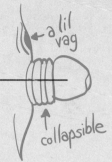

← a lil vag

collapsible

Butts are great and fuckable, but it's still hard to get past the poo part. So why not another non-poo orifice down there? Then you wouldn't have to make sex where poo comes from, I ... you're still going to do it aren't you? No matter how many holes I give you it's never enough, damn you! You'll always fuck the poo spot!

Also, butts should have nipples to play with.

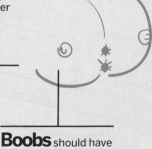

Boobs should have orifices too I guess.

TRUE TALES OF FIRST TIMES
from our erotic readers

"We get down to business, and he starts off weird with his hands down my pants, talking through it, and I'm internally snorting. Then, we're off to the races, and he gets ambitious and hits it from behind, but since he's totally wasted, he's fully pulling out and then missing. He's punching my taint and butt with his dick and I finally have to say, "Hey, not my ass." He lies down exhausted and says, "I think I'm a little too drunk... We can always try again in the morning." At this point I'm thinking to myself 'Gurl, get your ass out of there.' So, we settle into bed, and I'm still wide awake. I text my friend (since it was my first time) and she recommends I GTFO.

I surreptitiously get out of bed and try to put on my jeans without making noise. A quarter falls out of my pocket and bounces on the floor with a noise like a gunshot. He wakes up and asks where I'm going.

I say, "Oh, my...contacts are acting funny, I need to go take them out." He proceeds to walk me to the front door. Stark ass naked. And then gives me the most awkward hug of my life, while holding his junk in his poor little hand." **-Kelly**

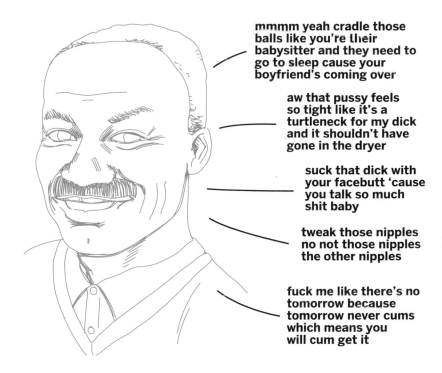

TRUE TALES OF FIRST TIMES
from our erotic readers

"He asked me to go with him to get some cigarettes so I hopped in his Chevette with Star Trek seat covers and we were off. We ended up parking in a gravel pit-like area. I admit it was in extremely poor judgment but I was 15 and for some reason I thought I was going to die soon and wanted to get this over with before that happened.

I had sex in the front seat of a Chevette with Star Trek seat covers with a guy in spandex shorts. Did I mention I'm 5'10"? This was no easy feat. We were interrupted by him being paged (remember pagers?) by his mom. He took me back to my cousin's boyfriend's house, but by then they'd left me there!

So there I was, stranded in a town 25 minutes away by car, recently fucked and fucked over, and left with a neck full of hickeys so bad it appeared as if I was strangled. And that's exactly what I lied to my mom when she had to pick me up. I told her that my cousin and I had been fighting and she strangled me and left me there." **-Missy**

HOW TO finger a butthole

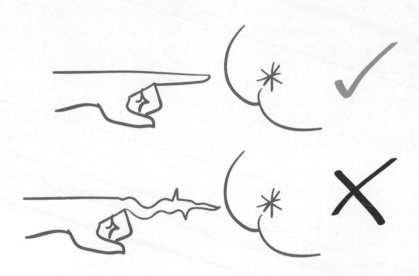

TRUE TALES OF FINDING
PORN from our erotic readers

"I was 12 when I stumbled across my first crumpled and damp book of wonder. It started in McDonalds and, well, that's also where it ends. I finished my Happy Meal and looked through the plastic leaves and branches of the fake shrubs that separated the booths. I looked through the leaves and saw a naked lady. A naked lady in McDonalds! Who takes porn to a McDonalds? Who leaves porn in a fake McDonalds hedge?! And why was it damp? WHY WAS IT DAMP?!" **-Scott**

"I came across a nude clipping in downtown Seattle. It was next to an I-5 offramp in SoDo and I saw it on my way to a Mariners game. Unfortunately, my dad was with me, so there wasn't much I could do beyond keep walking and pretend I didn't see it so as to avoid a terribly awkward conversation." **-Morgan**

HOT POSITIONS

the chocolate mckitten

Two poos becoming one is the ultimate act of intimacy, so much so that The Chocolate McKitten has become de rigueur as a replacement for traditional wedding vows.

e.t. the sex move

Also known as "Mac and Me: The Sex Move" when using Skittles.

queeps

Danger is a strong aphrodisiac, but remember to point the gun away from your partner when nearing climax, as it's all too common to pull the trigger when you cum.

HOT POSITIONS

brimping

The creators of "Gee, Your Hair Smells Terrific!" weren't stopping with shampoo: in 1976, the Gee Your Company Isn't Litigious corporation revealed this sexual possibility to coincide with the American bicentennial.

the candle in the wind

Created in tribute to the late Diana, Princess of Wales, who loved it so much she was known affectionately as "The Pee Pole's Princess." Did you know this book cannot be sold in the United Kingdom because of that joke?

the fleshy lightswitch

This fun move was created by Lighttube Flashlights to promote the flashlight as an erotic device. They went out of business when people confused them with "fleshlights," horribly cutting their penises.

TRUE TALES OF FINDING
PORN from our erotic readers

"My friends and I found a stash in the woods next to a creek. In panic and shame, we threw a copy of the Jenny McCarthy Playboy into the water. Months later, in the cold Ohio winter, we found that copy perfectly encapsulated in ice, like Mr. Freeze's wife; preserved forever in perfection in an icy coffin, never to survive warm hands again." **-Andy**

"My best friends and I discovered a treasure trove of torn pages of pornography. Being the wise old age of nine we spent WEEKS building a den deep in some bushes to house this treasure. We excavated a series of rooms to fully marvel at the majesty of our mucky books. The close proximity of the raw power of pornography eventually corrupted one of us and one day the stash was gone. Accusations flew but no one would admit to it. It looked like the mystery would never be solved until a week later when one of our group was no longer allowed out to play. Apparently they had taken the porn and hidden it on top of their shed, where it remained...until a big family BBQ, where, disturbed by a breeze, the pages had rained down upon the gathered masses." **-Richie**

MOVIE REVIEWS for all you sinephiles

THE SQUIRT LOCKER

Directed by Katherine Bigger-low
Starring F. Murray Gaybraham, Oliver Splatt, Paul Pooni

Even for pornography, this one was in really poor taste. And you'll need to take a Lactaid for all the prostate milking.

2.5 boners out of 10

POON

Directed by Duncan Bones
Starring Slam Cockswell

A lonely ass-tronaut, working alone on a moon base, hallucinates (or does he?) that he gets, like, so much space-ass. SO much. And then when he begins to hallucinate his twin (or does he), he/they double-team every moon-chick in space-sight.

7 boners out of 10

TRUE TALES OF FINDING PORN **from our erotic readers**

"As a kid I found an old, mostly-disintegrated porn magazine in the bush behind our house. All that was left was a softcore pictorial spread of a shy, young farm girl dressed in cutoffs, a knotted plaid shirt and sensible boots, holding a hatchet and chopping wood. I flipped the page and everything was still the same, except the shorts were gone, then the shirt; but thankfully, never the boots—safety first. And then the narrative really fell apart, and she was just holding an axe and fingering herself on top of a hay bale, and my confusion knew no bounds. That magazine left two indelible marks on me: I will always maintain that waist-down nudity is the least erotic of all, and that wood chopping will always affect me sexually."
-**Stephanie**

"My friend and I found porn at 14 when we were working at an amusement park. Amusement park parking lots have to be on par with the drive-in theater for places to have sex. Every day there were numerous used condoms littering the parking lot and once we even found a ridiculously large dildo." -**Jason**

TRUE TALES OF DOIN' IT
from our erotic readers

"I got a ring stuck while giving a blow job. I started choking. I was thinking, this is it. This is going to be how I die. Choked to death on cock. Death by weiner. I thought about my funeral and the people asking my mom how it happened.
I started laughing so hard at the absurdity of it all, that it came unstuck and all was well." **-Missy**

"I once lay down on the bed and told my husband to 'stick your man plunger in my lady toilet.' It didn't work for me, but I hold out hope for others." **-Rose**

"I once accidentally shot my own jizz in my mouth when I was masturbating, but I feel like that's probably happened to a lot of guys." **-Ryan**

SEX TIPS to make you best at sex

Dance like nobody's watching, have sex like your mother isn't there with you, constantly judging.

Sex with just the tip.

Make love, not war, and never to Gwar.

Role playing can help spice up your sex life. Pretend to be someone who's good at sex.

SEX TIPS

these will get you an a+ in sex college, even from cranky professor badsex

The sexiest part of the human body is the brain but do NOT crack your skull open during sex to test that out just trust me OK

The butthole can be a great source of pleasure and poo.

Buy more fruits & vegetables. I heard the guy who works at the fruits & vegetables place gives super beejays.

Nipple clamps are excellent for keeping nipples in place.

SEX TIPS

for those times when you're having sex and want it to not be the worst

When there was only one pair of footprints that's when you were just crazy bouncin' on my big ol' rod.

| Have sex with me please.

1. Stick it in.
2. Wiggle it around.
3. NAILED IT

| Butt stuff.

SEX TIPS

these will make your partner go 'mmm' and 'ohhh' and 'whaaaat' guaranteed i guess

Ladies—is your man "ready" to "go"? Grab it hard and sing all of "Blue Christmas" into it. That'll chill him the fuck out.

Alien on the streets, Predator in the sheets.

Fellas—are you "ready" to "go"? Well watch out 'cause I heard your girl likes grabbing dicks and singing Christmas songs into 'em for some fucking reason.

You need to change your safeword every three weeks for security reasons and it must have numbers in it.

EROTICA erotiCAN not erotiCAN'T

Marvin was reluctant. Terry tried to ease his mind.

"Come on, man. I sucked you. Now you just have to suck me. No biggie." Terry undid his jeans, casually, like it was no biggie.

Marvin was still pretty unsure. He DID enjoy being sucked, so it seemed only fair to return the favor. But what awaited him in his good buddy's denim tool chest? He kneeled down and gingerly pulled down Terry's discount underwear, shocked at what he found.

"It's a penis! Just like mine!" Marvin squealed. "Ha ha! Fantastic! I love my penis! This is such a great opportunity to engage another penis! Yay!"

Marvin gobbled the shit out of it, just went to town, cause how often does someone who HAS a penis get to play with ANOTHER one? What a wonderful thing.

Terry smiled. Everything was going according to his plan to cum.

SEX TIPS

you can't go wrong with these, but this statement is not legally binding

Nothing wrong with stopping at second base for the first few weeks. But if you were a pro baseball player I'd fucking fire you.

Handjobs are a nice way of letting him know that you're not enjoying this screening of "Her."

Do NOT refer to your sexual partner as an "all-you-can-eat buffet" OR as a "late night Taco Bell drive-thru."

Pretend to be a sexy firefighter and just be constantly distracted that you'll be called to fight a fire while making love.

SEX TIPS

these will really spice things up in the boudoir (french bedroom)

"You unlock many more back doors with a finger than with a fist."
-Ancient Common Fucking Sense

Eat the rich, yes, but also eat the poor. Your tongue should know no socio-economic bounds.

Do not refer to your partner's vagina as: Baby Sleeve, The Good Sarlaac, Meat Vault, The Asshole's Companion, Downton Alley, The Uncanny Valley, Ms. Nasty's School For Boys, The Holistic Healer, The Matrimonial Hole, Sandra, Number 36, Vag of Honor, Boner Hotel, Mystic Pizza, Natural Fleshlight

FAMOUS DONGS
great peenies throughout history

"foreskin +7 inches to go"

THE BUNT

When early baseball legend Dickey Pearce took a pitch low and inside to the penis, resulting in a fair ball tapped gently into play down the third base line, the national pastime was forever changed. As was Dickey Pearce's penis.

THE RAIL SPLITTER

The great emancipator of Abraham Lincoln, 16th President of the United States, once was used as a sundial to help Gen. Ulysses S. Grant commence military action at Vicksburg.

THE COON SKIN CAP

Tennessee senator Estes Kefauver's notorious "subcommittee member" terrorized Washington DC during the 1950s.

THE CANADIAN IN HOLLYWOOD

How do YOU measure up to beloved television actor Raymond Burr, star of PERRY MASON and IRONSIDE?

GANDALF THE GREY

In THE TWO TOWERS, novelist J.R.R. Tolkien reveals that Odinic wanderer Gandalf's "life-staff when twiddled could I daresay extend out past the length of half a fort-moss worth of an elf's noodle," or about four inches.

"you shall not pass hot ass"

JUSTICE RUTH BADER GINSBURG

This associate justice of the Supreme Court of the United States has had to serve on the bench next to William Rehnquist, Antonin Scalia, Clarence Thomas, and others—so the next time you want to complain about YOUR shitty co-workers, take a note from Justice G and man up, buttercup.

SEX TIPS for love having

Stare deep into his eyes during sex. Then afterwards. Then watch him sleep. Watch him wake, watch him eat. Don't blink. Don't move. Ever again. His orgasm will be thanks enough.

Move as if you're in slow motion during love making. Slow your pulse. Lower your body temperature. Hibernate.

Just like in the commercials for boner medicine, lug two goddamn claw-foot bathtubs up a fucking mountain and stare at a meadow or something.

Looking to explore anal sex? Get a funny little miner's hat, with a light on it! And maybe a little toy pick-axe.

SEX TIPS

fun at parties which prominently feature fucking

Have sex while standing up (for the rights of gays & lesbians to marry their partners).

A fun, sexy tattoo for guys would be to make it look like your penis is a strap-on.

Do not refer to your partner's penis as: Hmm Interesting, Sexual Gary Jr., Tickle Stick, Mr. Nuisance, The Crying Noodle, Stinkpeen, Adorable, Wubby Nubby, Is It In, Discount Hot Dog, Non-Detachable Dildo, Non-Vibrating Dildo, Dildo That Suddenly Becomes Soft, Cute Li'l Thing, Ha Ha Ha

SEX TIPS

drive them WILD in bed with these hot tips until you have to call animal control on them

If she doesn't want to go down on you, try improving the taste of your semen by eating watermelon, celery, her pussy.

Pre-ejaculate is nature's lubricant, so feel free to drag your freshly erect penis along your bike chain every few months.

Remember, slow and steady wins the race. And it IS a race. Never forget that if you want to be a winner.

Feet are EXTREMELY sexy and should be paid attention to in bed. Oh, also, did you know Quentin Tarantino is a foot fetishist, I—wait, where are you

SEX TIPS
these are not meant to arouse you, just educate you, OK?

Denying your partner satisfaction can be a real turn-on for both of you. Blindfold them, tease them with light touches and then move to a new city.

Don't feel bad if your partner needs to touch themself and your best friend in order to get off.

Having sex in new locations can be exciting, like when Neil Armstrong fucked the moon.

Shower sex is great because you can fantasize that you're having sex out in the rain but the rain is hot because these are the End Times.

HOT POSITIONS

bloobing

Bloobing was outlawed in 1978 in the UK when people started doing it as a dance move in Euroclubs.

swaffling

70% of women who have swaffled report that they feel "comforted" by the move and that it makes them feel like a "sexy basketball," which is a top fantasy.

reverse-reverse cowgirl

This bold move was invented in 1986 by Jerry Tankworth, a very lazy man who felt great claustrovaginalphobia when performing a traditional "69" pose.

TRUE TALES OF
WET DREAMS from our erotic readers

"I thought that I would tell you about my first 'wet dream.'
I was about 11 or 12 when it happened and in the dream I was
at a pool party. I saw some girl sitting in the hot tub who was a
little bit older, i.e. 13 or 14, i.e. desirable, so I approached her
and we started talking. I don't remember what was said, but it
must have gone well because we didn't even leave the hot tub
for a more private place, I was just vigorously humping her in
clear daylight. At first, she was enjoying it quite well, so I kept
on going. However, as we went on, the expression on her face
slowly turned into one of horrified disgust.

I stopped and asked her what was wrong before she replied,
'It's ok, most guys shit themselves when they hump me.' I
awake immediately to realize that I had indeed just pooped
myself. It was really awkward too because I was on vacation
with my family and I was sharing a bed with my brother."
-William

TRUE TALES OF FINDING
PORN from our erotic readers

"The weaseliest kid in my grade 7 class somehow got his unworthy little hands on a new-car-smell issue of Penthouse, and told the rest of us that he'd show it to us in the woods behind the school over the lunch break.

Six or seven 13-year-old boys descended on the woods. The fight lasted about 45 seconds, in which all of us—nerds every last one—fought each other like animals for right and title to a single article of pornography, with not a single word spoken, except by the poor kid who'd brought the magazine in the first place, who tried to talk us out of it, while we destroyed his prize, and ourselves.

The Penthouse was ripped into so many pieces in the course of that fight that to this day, I remember the ass and labia of a lady against the clear blue sky, but have no idea what her body or face looked like above the waist, because she'd been bisected through the midsection. I hung on to that shred, and a few others, limped home bleeding and hid them under my mattress, until I worked out that taping them to the underside of my sock drawer was way smarter." -**Matt**

SEX TIPS
these'll do the trick

Stage a hot rendezvous in a hotel room. Use an assumed name. Rent a car unlike your own. Drive an unpredictable route. Arrive at a time long past when you'd normally be asleep. Your name is now NORMAN SUGGS. The ID is in the bedside table. "The package" will arrive at 6 AM. Be ready. Be brave. The revolution will never forget you, "Norman Suggs."

While gently kissing her clitoris, hire a barbershop quartet to serenade you. They should be in the room with you. You know why? Chicks. Dig. Sleeve. Garters.

Gay men know the secret to great oral sex: put his penis in your mouth.

we spin alone

in great swaths
of darkness

a seemingly
uncaring cosmos

but we are all united
by the strands
of energy

woven through
space

woven through
time

captured
and framed

through the universal act
of sex

THE SOLAR SYSTEM

Paint your partner's butt to look like outer space and watch it gobble up our precious anal planets! But watch out for Saturn's rings!

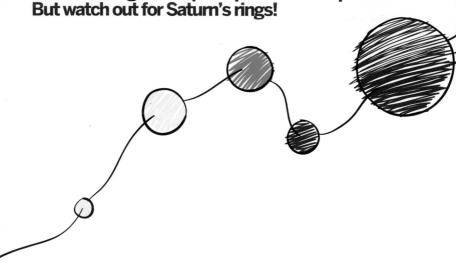

MOVIE REVIEWS

netflix for your netdix
v.o.d. for your v.a.g.

ALL THAT JIZZ

Directed by Rod Fosse
Starring Boy Schneider

Maniacal film director directs this porno about a maniacal director directing a porno about a maniacal porno director directing a porno. Ben Vereen shows up in the end and really needs a new agent.

9 boners out of 10

TEENAGE NUDIST NINJA TURTLES

Directed by Michael Lay
Starring voices and computers

These turtles are all like, "fuck shells" and let it all hang out, attracting a lot of turtle-curious poontang let me tell you. See Michael Hang So Low, Dong A Fellow, Spaffael and Leonarblo just go fuck crazy in your sewers.

10 boners out of 10

SEX TIPS

Remember this simple mnemonic: "Stuck in a rut? Thumb in the butt. Need to slow down? Grab your cock and punch it as hard as you can."

"Crossing your fingers" has a 0% birth control effectiveness rate, but I don't know, maybe this time...?

Remember this simple mnemonic: "Feelin' kinky? Stick in a pinky! Feelin' romantic? Grab your cock and punch it as hard as you can."

Fellas! Want to drive her wild? Then learn how to fold a goddamn bath towel, Gerry, jesus FUCK

TRUE TALES OF DOIN' IT
from our erotic readers

"Usually what would happen is at around 6AM (I live in DC, so everyone wakes up early) whichever guy I had the one-night stand with would kick me awake and tell me to leave because they had to go to work. What was different about this one was that not only did I wake up on my own, but I woke up to the smell of him making breakfast. Like, the sex was pretty alright, but this literally made it the best one-night stand I had ever had. So, to properly thank him, I get under his apron while he's still fixing breakfast. And of course, when he was moving the sausages from the pan to a plate, he accidentally spilled hot grease on my back. It didn't burn or anything, but it was still a jolt, so my first instinct is to bite down.

"At first, I thought that must've really done it for him, because I feel my mouth filling up with something. Then I realized it tasted like pennies. I immediately spit out a mouthful of blood and look up to see this horrid, pained look on his face. He's grabbing around for a towel and I'm in a panic, and he's telling me to go brush my teeth because they're bloodstained. We then plan going to the hospital, which is an ordeal in itself, because we're not going on the metro, because he has a towel wrapped around his dick and can't fit it in his pants. I didn't drive at all, and he's not a super-confident driver (also the bleeding dick part probably didn't help), so he has to have both hands on the wheel, which means I have to hold the towel in place and provide pressure. So, the cars passing us by that day must've seen something that looked a lot more fun than it was. When we get to the hospital, he insists to do all the talking because my teeth are still bloodstained. What I had done was torn the vein on the top of his dick with my teeth. He needed immediate surgery and stitches, as well as to be on half dose Viagra that would keep him semi-erect at all times, because if he was too erect the stitches would tear, but if he was too limp they wouldn't hold in place. Which also means he had to get a penis cast." -**Dennis**

"I was dating this girl who loved Van Morrison's 'Brown-Eyed Girl' waaay more than a 17-year old should in 1998. She thought it would be fun to 'make love in the green grass'. So one night, we decided to do it outside, and what better place than in my parents' side yard?

"That was how I found out I had a pretty serious grass allergy." -**David**

SEX TIPS

these will for sure get you a marriage proposal or a divorce, whichever floats your boat.

BDSM stands for BONDAGE DISCIPLINE SPIDER-MAN.

Ladies! Looking to blow his mind in bed? Invent a time machine in bed.

If you're with a man who finishes too quickly, whisper "99% of all pregnancies are caused by sex" to slow him down.

If you have trouble getting it up, draw tiny balls on your knuckles and pretend your fingers are dicks

SEX TIPS try these out I guess

Try making love while fucking. It's tricky, like rubbing your belly and patting your head simultaneously.

Rub your belly and pat your head simultaneously before having sex so you can impress your partner with your physical multitasking.

Eat a lot of protein before sex, like a cold can of beans or a bowl of Cum Flakes™.

A lot of women rely on their own touch for orgasm during sex, so make sure to give her some space for this. Go for a walk around the block or something.

SEX TIPS

don't forget to have sex

Cross-dressing can really spice things up. Ladies, try wearing a man's dress shirt and tie to bed. Men, try wearing high heels and a skirt and thousands of years of patriarchal oppression to bed.

Try out some sexy board games in the boudoir. Don't have any? Sex-convert existing ones! Like Settlers of Dat Ass, Bi-opoly, Frisk, Battledick, Trivial Fursuit, Connect Foursome, Baby Got Backgammon, Chesst

Have sex outside, in the middle of Yankee Stadium, during a game.

PICK-UP LINES

'cause those always work, yeah?

Hey girl, do you like to fuck? If yes, I may have a follow-up question or two, I guess.

Ooh, boy, are you an ice cream cone? 'Cause I'd sure like to lick you and feel sick and regretful later.

Ooh, boy, are you Hannibal? 'Cause I want you to eat me and also to be Mads Mikkelsen, who is far more attractive than you are.

Ooh, boy. Are you a fireman? No? Oh, sorry, I'm only into firemen.

Hey girl, are you NASA's space program? 'Cause a nation wants to start you up again.

Hey girl, are you my mother 'cause—oh god, did I just say that—

Hey girl, are you on LinkedIn? 'Cause I'd endorse you for "being fine." I—oh, you're not? Well, its a social networking site with a focus on wor—

Ooh, boy. Are you a rocket ship cow? 'Cause I want to get inside you and milk you.

SEX TIPS

master these before you turn the page

Push each other to your limits during sex, not just physically, but mentally as well, asking each other really tricky math problems.

The best sex is Vacation sex. Pop in that Chevy Chase classic and go to town.

Candles can really set the mood, so pop a couple in your butthole.

Bring your partner close to orgasm but then pull back. Repeat this move until they divorce you.

EROTICA to read in a haunted house or on a haunted bus

"**W**hat're you so scared of? Afraid a ghost will slap your ding dong?" Karen really knew how to get Johnny's goat. She shouldn't have been so mean since Johnny had only agreed to rub one out in Old Man McGarnickle's Haunted House because it was HER fetish.

"Pfft. I ain't afraid of no ghost." Johnny lay back on the creaky, dry and eager floor and whipped out 'Medium Johnny.' "I'll cum all over this dumb house. I don't care."

Johnny stroked and stroked like a good boy. Chills ran down his spine as he was about to strike midnight on the ol' spurt clock. Did he just hear a wolf moan at the moon? Did that painting on the wall just lick its lips? He pushed on through his terror and dribbled out a bunch of his stuff, satisfying his erotic mandate. Just then, Karen hauled off and slapped his freshly expunged peener.

"What the hell, Karen? What was that for?"

"Oh, sweet Johnny, don't you get it?" Karen grinned.

"I'm a ghost."

ASK THE SEXPERTS

"Where is the clitoris?" -Derek

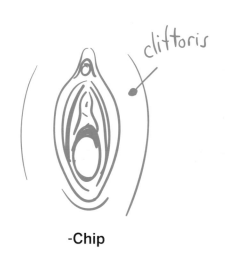

clittoris

-Chip

-Matt

SEX TIPS

because this book is called just the tips, remember?

Talk dirty with excellent enunciation. Nobody likes Mr. Mumbles in the boudoir, chum.

Why are sexy costumes relegated to Halloween? Surprise your partner with Sexy Easter Bunny and Sexy Arbor Day.

Read your partner the sexiest story ever told: the story of Noah's Ark. It's literally about every species on the planet fucking! For survival!

Guys, most ladies enjoy seeing their man-partners pleasuring themselves. So that disappointed look she's giving you in the restaurant is probably just her role-playing or something.

SEX TIPS
so you can sex better until you're the best sexer

If he says he wants to watch porno with you, go for it. It can be a great way to start things up. But if he hits play on My Little Pony get the fuck out of there.

It's fun to have sex in the bath! You can pretend you're Aquaman except you're getting laid.

A man's testicles are very sensitive and some sex moves can hurt them a bit, so just poke them back up inside his body where they'll be safe.

Some guys can only orgasm through a sense of commitment and love so just pop the question already!

SEX TIPS
to make you the belle of the ball(s)

Looking to "spice" things up? Cook up something kinky for him in the kitchen! Like a banana with a vagina, or maybe a casserole, but with a vagina! Or maybe just some fruit boobs.

Ever try role-playing in the bedroom? Pretend you're a randy druid looking for some hot chaotic-neutral elf action before winter's solstice and the return of the ninth age of the dragonborn.

The one sex move guaranteed to drive him wild? Manipulate his penis until he ejaculates. You can use your hand, mouth, lady-business, or really pretty much anything. Just, y'know. It's pretty easy. Men. Eesh.

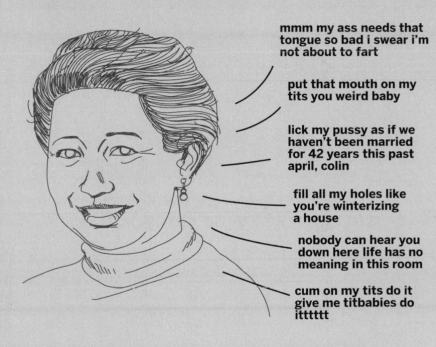

HOT POSITIONS

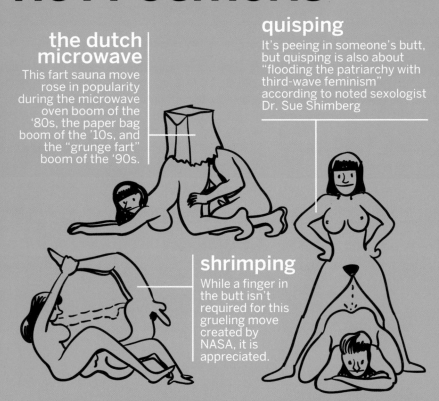

the dutch microwave

This fart sauna move rose in popularity during the microwave oven boom of the '80s, the paper bag boom of the '10s, and the "grunge fart" boom of the '90s.

quisping

It's peeing in someone's butt, but quisping is also about "flooding the patriarchy with third-wave feminism" according to noted sexologist Dr. Sue Shimberg

shrimping

While a finger in the butt isn't required for this grueling move created by NASA, it is appreciated.

HOW TO give a handjob

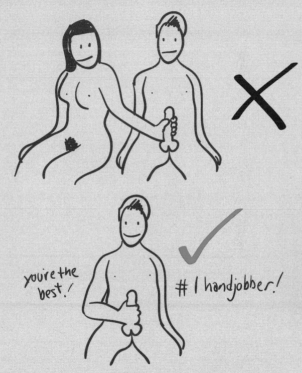

EROTICA to read to criminals

Bruce heard the feral noises from inside his parents'
bedchamber and couldn't help but steal a glance inside,
and the strange new yearning in his pantsal region
compelled him to keep staring. Jose, one of the men that
tended the family grounds, eagerly serviced Bruce's
mother as Bruce's father drew obscene arabesques
across the man's back with the tip of his own erect
manservant. Just like Zorro, Bruce thought, as Jose's
criado scattered a fine strand of pearls across his
screaming mother's neck, just like Zorro.

As his father's alfred spewed frothy white pleasantries of
its own, Bruce felt extraordinary warmth inside his gut,
followed by something rapidly cooling down his leg —
he'd wet himself. Letting it go, Bruce whimpered just
loud enough to betray his presence to his post-coital
parents and their randy shrubsman. As the adults
approached the door calling after him, Bruce ran.

Telltale drops of urine like little yellow footprints led his
naked and glistening parents to him as young Bruce

forced his way through the massive doors of his stately manor. Running across the grounds as fast as he could, Bruce's parents right behind him, the boy felt alive and free and wet and pee-soaked, really really pee-soaked, for the first time in his life.

He became aware, after a time, that he was alone. His parents no longer gave chase. Wandering back towards the mansion, Bruce found his parents dead at the bottom of a bat-infested sinkhole on the property. Jose wept at the sinkhole's edge, praying to a god that would not respond.

Bruce beat Jose to death with a fire poker, the first of many in lower socioeconomic classes than his own that he would punish for his parents' death that day.

"Yes father," said Bruce. "I shall become a bat."

HOT POSITIONS

the swift gary

Headbutt the tip of your partner's erect peener. It probably feels really good!

the '80s sitcom

Have your partner burst through the front door, smile, and then freeze while you give him a beejer! Relieve those "growing pains" in his "small wonder!"

butt nugging

Let your partner scoot across the floor while anal beads pop out. Their destination can be to fetch more anal beads!

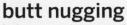

ASK THE SEXPERTS

"What's the worst thing either of you have done trying to get sex?"

Fingerbanging Amy Barnes really, really poorly at the movies, maybe? -**Matt**

Pretending to be Amy Barnes that one time. -**Chip**

"What's the most visually appealing way of trimming/styling pubic hair for ladies?"

An Aladdin Sane lightning bolt. -**Matt**

Shave it all off and glue it back to your body one inch to the left and two inches higher. -**Chip**

SEX TIPS
to last you all winter long

When you blow him, try actually blowing. His tum-tum will inflate to adorable proportions!

Blindfold him! Tie his wrists to the bedposts! Take the car! Take the credit cards! Drive like the wind, Melissa! DRIVE LIKE THE WIND. YOU ARE A BEAUTIFUL FREE MAJESTIC EAGLE NOW MELISSA.

Elbow-length opera gloves add a splash of old-money pizzazz to your next hand job at the opera.

Next time he's standing "at attention," get a tasty donut and stick his member through the hole. Take his picture. Send to everyone he works with. Guys love that. Guys seriously super love that.

SEX TIPS
for the discerning fucker

Spice up his hours at the office by faxing him your panties.

After a long day at work, draw her a hot bath, make a cup of her favorite herbal tea, and then fuck the living shit out of her. She might just thank you for it!

Flirting with strangers on trains can be hot! Also dangerous. Also like super super dangerous.

Trying on clothes? Send him naughty snapshots from inside the dressing room that you've had done by a professional photographer and make-up artist team, arranged ahead of time. Then fuck the photographer and make-up artist team.

HOT POSITIONS

bloobing

"The milky hot dog," aka "titty fucking," is a time-honored tradition, enhanced by this robust move. A nice touch is to paint nipples on the male's buttocks, so the participating lady can feel like she's rimming beautiful, stinky breasts.

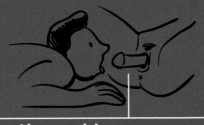

turtle sucking

A double-ended dildo can be a world of fun, and one of its countries is "turtle sucking," where you insert it halfway into your hoo-ha and your partner performs oral sex on it, but bites down and pushes it in and out mmm yeah

female injaculation

Instead of squirting at the moment of climax, spit on your partner's face! A fun surprise!

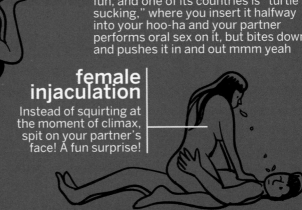

MOVIE REVIEWS
two thumbs up where? fantastic!

SKYBALLS

Directed by Sam Bendes
Starring George Glazenby, Pussy Pleasefuckithard, Todger Moore

The origin of 0069, James Bang, at long last revealed, while a bisexual psychopath lays waste to the Scottish countryside: his mom and dad died and he hid in a hole. Beautifully shot by Roger Freakins.

6 boners out of 10

PINEAPPLE SEXPRESS

Directed by David Porndon Cream
Starring Sex Brogen, James Spanko, Danny Dick Pride

Two good friends smoke a humongous joint and tag team a pineapple. But they're so high they don't realize the pineapple is actually their pal Danny who is totally cool with this whole thing.

7 boners out of 10

MEASURE YOUR PEENER
very accurately

1" — You are a baby! You shouldn't be reading this! You—wait a second. H-how can a baby read? AH! WITCH BABY! BURN THE WITCH BABY!

2" — But it looks SUPER-thick though.

3" — Oh, it's not that bad. There's oral sex and fingers and fists and dildos and becoming the CEO of a major corporation.

4" — You can at least shout "I'M THE FANTASTIC FOUR" when you make sex.

5" — The average penis size is between five and six inches, so with this length you can describe yourself as an "everyman" in your online profile.

6" — It does an honest day's work for an honest buck.

(This "slightly off" measuring scale will make your manjunk seem larger, but remember to cover this portion with your thumb before taking the picture and sending it to your constituents!)

Unnecessarily large, imo.

Man, must hurt that it's just not quite a foot long, eh? Watch this ONE COOL TRICK to gain an EXTRA INCH.

Big enough that you may just let your other skills lapse, like oral sex, foreplay, driving, showering, etc.

Wow! Do you have a permit for that? I mean, I really hope you do because I'm pretty sure walking around with your dick hanging out of your pants is illegal.

It's pretty good, but really it's just 0.00012263 miles so don't get all conceited.

Chip's penis is 6.75" long, so you have the same length penis of a very sad NYT bestselling dildo drawer!

12"

11"

10"

9"

8"

7"

SEX TIPS

look, it's time you figured this shit out. we can't hold your hand forever

Ladies! Write down something you wish he'd do to you. Leave it under his pillow. After you make the bed. Again. Y'know what, to hell with him.

Ladies! Leave a sexy pair of panties in his glove compartment. If he finds them, pretend you have no idea whose they are or how they got there. Watch him squirm. It'll be hilarious.

Fellas! Like when she waxes it? You fucking try it, buddy. It's no party. And if she does wax it for you? You better go down like Peter McNeeley.

Peter McNeeley was a no-name boxer Mike Tyson knocked down twice in the first two minutes of a fight.

HOW TO leave porn in the woods

MOVIE REVIEWS

MANSCATTIN'

Directed by Wood E. Allen
Starring Wood E. Allen, Dianne Freakin', Tony Roberts

Fifty-something nebbish can't figure out why his witty klatsch of urbane friends feel repulsed by his desire to feast on the shit of his fifteen-year-old girlfriend. Bouncy but inappropriate score.

5 boners out of 10

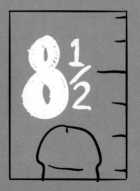

8½

Directed by Federico Fullpeenie
Starring Marcello Mastriboni

A self-obsessed and well-endowed director struggles to think of a title for his new film, all about his almost-nine-inch penis, as his cast and crew bone lazily in the Italian countryside. Also, dreams?

8½ boners out of 10

SEX TIPS

for an ok time

Massage is a great way to connect to one another physically as well as spiritually. Devote your life to studying Ayurvedic massage, the traditional Hindu system of medicine. Become Hindu. Move to Bangalore. Jerk him off in Bangalore.

Connect to your mate by feeling their heartbeat and pulse during lovemaking. Many EKG readers and blood pressure monitors are covered in velvet, fur, and other sensual, medically accurate textures.

Lesbians! Looking to take it beyond scissoring? Try rocking, which always beats scissoring, or papering, which is even better than rocking.

SEX TIPS

If you find you don't have time during your busy day for sex then start having microsex while you go for coffee or fold laundry. Just super tiny sex.

Spice things up by using a vacuum cleaner during sex if your fetish is emergency rooms.

Join the "mile-high" club and fuck an airplane.

Ladies! When faking your orgasms, don't forget to contrive a convincing backstory and family history for each, just in case he quizzes you later.

EROTICA for the dark recesses of your sex tunnels

Gary stepped into the dark club, like a newborn fawn, slimy and weak. A woman approached him. Her blonde hair was like golden wheat, but not dry and lifeless like Farmer Miller's wheat. It was like wet wheat, cascading over her fair features like a tumultuous wheat river. She smiled at him, but he was taken aback at the copious amount of blood dripping from her mouth.

"Oh! I know what you're thinking, but this isn't blood!" She said while baring her ivory teeth, lightly dappled with red like a bad spatter paint job my mother would have attempted on our living room in the '90s. "It's a way of life!"

She took one look at Gary in his leather diaper and knew what he needed. "You're a bad baby, aren't you?"

Gary turned and hiked down his diappy, revealing a tattoo of his arrest record for tax evasion.

"The baddest baby." Gary smirked as he said this. The woman nodded. It was going to be a hell of a night.

DIRTY TALK

counterprogramming to the summer blockbuster "dirty action"

I love you. God, how I love you. Every morning I wake up and feel your warm body against mine and wonder how did I ever live before you? Your smell, your smile, the way you brush away your hair behind your ear when you're shy. Every lovely and loving gesture you make is etched onto my soul. We understand each other on a level that makes our every touch feel predestined. Making love to you is the most perfect thing I'm a part of. And all I can do is thank you.

Cork my ass with that giant cock you filthy blessing!

THE
END

has an abundance
of nerve endings
and can be
incorporated
safely into your
sexual lifestyle.
Goodbye.

**Matt Fraction
is sorry, mom.**

**Chip Zdarsky
is 38 years old with over 19
years of fucking experience,
but not necessarily in a row.
He is not a doctor, but he can
still get rubber gloves
wholesale.**

**Together they are the
creators of the award-winning
comic book SEX CRIMINALS
through Image Comics.**